CW01551199

The **London Challenge**
For world class education

London Challenge Design Collaborative

Re-engaging Disaffected Students in Learning
Booklet One : Sharing Our Learning
May 2005

Written and collated by Professor Kathryn Riley, Institute of Education, University of London

Project Team : Kathryn Riley (Team Leader), Sherry Hallmond, Jason Johnson, Kay Smith, Jean Seddon and Wendy Weinstock.

Collaborating Schools : Greenwich (Eltham Green, Kidbrooke and Thomas Tallis), Hammersmith and Fulham (Burlington Danes, Bridge Academy and Henry Compton).

Partner Institute : Margaret McMillan House, Outdoor Education Centre, Kent (Stephen Ellis and James Tarrant).

Project Steering Group: Nick Brenton (ALCEO), Madelaine Caplin (Greenwich), Anna Paige (London Challenge), Dinesh Ramjee (Henry Compton School), Rob Thomas (Thomas Tallis School), Les Thompson (Hammersmith and Fulham).

Published by: Thomas Tallis School, Kidbrooke Park Road, London SE3 9PX
Designed by: Jean Cripps
Printed by: Kleur Media

ISBN: 0-9550485-0-8

Re-engaging Disaffected Students in Learning

Re-engaging Disaffected Students in Learning is an innovative two year research and development project, funded as part of the London Challenge. It began in 2004 and involves six London secondary schools, three in Greenwich (Eltham Green, Kidbrooke and Thomas Tallis) and three in Hammersmith and Fulham (Burlington Danes[1], Bridge Academy and Henry Compton). Margaret McMillan House (MMH) Outdoor Education Centre, Kent is a key partner in the project and we have had support from sixth form mentors from the Greenwich Schools and from William Morris Academy, Hammersmith and Fulham.

In this booklet, the first from the project, we describe what the project has set out to do, how we've gone about it, and what we have learned so far. We concentrate on the general approach, the research tools and staff and students' expectations about the project. As the booklet is intended for professional development purposes, please feel free to photocopy.

We are still only part way through our journey and would love to hear from you.

- What do you think about the project and the direction we're taking?

- Are you doing anything similar?

- Would you like to be kept in touch about future developments?

Email us at: s.kay@thomastallis.greenwich.sch.uk

[1] Burlington Danes will join the project in September 2005.

introduction

What we are aiming to do, and how have we gone about it?

our journey

Starting Points

Most children start schools with enthusiasm and curiosity. What changes for some of them and why? In this project we are trying to identify what turns students off learning. Why do some students become disengaged? Why do they drift through their school years? And perhaps even more importantly, what can be done to re-engage them in learning?

Our approach

Over recent years, a number of initiatives have focused on disaffected students. We wanted to learn from these but also to look afresh, by trying to see things from different perspectives: the young people themselves, their families and the staff who work with them. Our project consultant, Kathryn Riley, had led work in Lancashire which had a look at student disaffection from those different vantage points. (See *Working with Disaffected Students: Why students lose interest in schools and what we can do about it,* K Riley and E Rustique-Forrester, 2002, London: Chapman Sage > www.sagepub.co.uk). We wanted to put some of those ideas into practice and to experiment further.

Our immediate goal is to make a real and tangible difference to students in the six schools involved in the project. We want to raise their aspirations, increase their self-esteem and help them to achieve. We also want to share our learning with other schools.

We began with three basic working hypotheses which have informed how we have gone about the project.

Hypothesis 1 : It ain't what you do, it's the way that you do it

If we start by viewing disaffected students not as problems to be sorted, but as change agents, they will provide new insights into how marginalised students can become re-engaged in learning.

Hypothesis 2 : It 's all about learning, relationship and mutual respect

- Schooling is often a fragmented, disconnected and inconstant experience for many children and young people on the margins. Any change and improvement strategy aimed at making a difference to their experience of education will need to focus on learning: new ways of learning and new contexts for learning.
- Relationships between students and school staff are important for most students, but particularly so for students on the margins. Creating opportunities for students and staff to develop meaningful relationships is a critical part of the change process

Hypothesis 3 : Staff need support, time and opportunities

- Most school staff want to make a positive difference to the lives of their students. But if things are to change for disaffected students, staff will need time, tools and opportunities to look at students' experiences in new ways, and chances to work together in collaborative arrangements which take them beyond their classrooms and school gates.

What's in it for students?

Students told us that they signed up for the project because...

I knew that this challenge could help me in my learning and to get along with people which I've had problems with.

I thought it would be about group work.

I was happy coz my mates were in it.

Dunno...I can get out of my lessons.

I was excited because it was different.

I thought it would be fun.

Wow cool!

I thought it was a good thing because I could spend time with teachers I could trust.

student quotesstudent quotesstudent quotes

our journey

Eltham Green Girls

Our approach has included six steps along the way...

steps along the way

Step I : Identify a core team of staff who want to explore new ways of working with students and develop a change strategy

Nuts and Bolts: We began by asking each participating school to nominate a research and action team of teachers and learning mentors. To support these teams, and the project's overall development, a Core Project Team was set up which included a Project Consultant (Professor Kathryn Riley), an administrator (Kay Smith) and two borough-based researchers (Sherry Hallmond and Wendy Weinstock). Two full-time learning mentors (Jason Johnson and Jean Seddon) were also appointed to join the team and work directly with schools. A project steering group has oversight of the project and members of the core team meet regularly with lead staff from the six schools and from Margaret McMillan House (MMH) Outdoor Education Centre, Kent, Stephen Ellis and James Tarrant.

Each school team has identified a cohort of between 10-15 students to take part in the project. In the first year of the project, September 2004-July 2005, the teams are using a range of tools and approaches to:

- Examine how disaffected students experience their learning;
- Develop a range of strategies to improve learning opportunities; and
- Share their learning with colleagues in their own schools, partner schools and other schools.

Each school team has also developed its own school-based strategy to work directly with students and parents. All of the students are participating in a range of learning opportunities at Margaret McMillan House. The focus of the second year of the project

(September 2005-July 2006) will be on how to transfer this learning into the school curriculum, and into schools' day-to-day practices. Our approach can be summarised as follows:

- Develop collaboration;
- Identify barriers and gateways to learning;
- Build aspirations and expectations;
- Involve groups in the change process;
- Share learning at every stage;
- Identify new approaches to teaching and learning which will improve the classroom and school environment.

Step 2 : Give staff time to share their aspirations

At the end of June 2004 we held our first residential workshop, joined by staff from Wigan who are involved in a parallel project. At the workshop, participants were asked to design an 'aspirational' poster which identified what they hoped to achieve through the project: what changes did they want in their schools and for young people?

A number of common themes and images ran through these posters. The shared goal was to move away from the negative experiences which shroud schooling for many disaffected students: from situations in which students felt stuck, powerless, misunderstood or full of rage, to ones in which they are listened to. Trust was needed to build new relationships and create alternative sets of expectations (see poster 1). Workshop participants saw this as moving from a 'Why should I?' culture to one which generated confidence, excitement, purpose, engagement and achievement: 'Dream it, Be it, Learn it, Share it' was the slogan for one poster. The aspirational posters contained positive words and images: sunshine and smiles, openness and sharing (see poster 2).

Give staff time to share their aspirations...

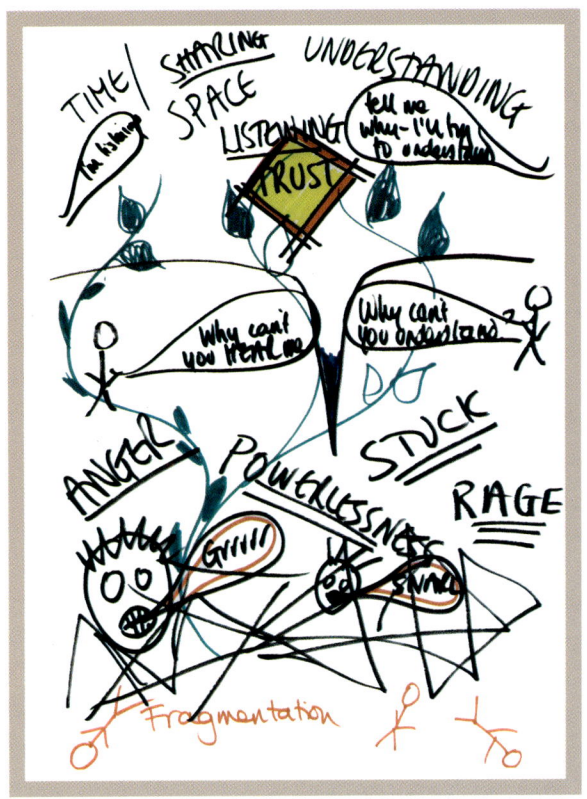

Staff Poster 1 : From Powerlessness to Trust

Staff Poster 2 : School - the place to be

steps along the way

steps along the way

Step 3 : Give staff opportunities to experiment with a range of research tools and work together

The school teams were offered a range of research tools to look at students' experience in new ways. These included:

- Being a student for a day;
- Using a questionnaire framework and focus group discussions with parents, students or staff, or with all three groups and trying to compare views;
- Using students' drawings as a way of enabling them to describe their school experience in a different way.

When they came together at our first residential workshop, they shared their learning from their research activities.

Student for a day

- *You look at the school environment in a different way and notice different things, including the posters and the messages ('Do listen to your Teacher' 'Be the Best you can Be')* **and what** *makes teachers tired or angry.*
- *An interesting activity but there are problems about being an adult observer and issues about how you interpret a situation.*
- *What happens at break-time can be as important as, or even more important than, what happens in the classroom.*
- *Some useful insight into what students are required to do:*
  - *> Students are wearied by the emphasis on writing tasks;*
  - *> There can be certain pressurised situations which lead to stress and create, for example, regular headaches for students.*
- *There are opportunities for students to use this as a research tool, reflecting on what they see and experience in other schools.*

Focus Groups

- *Face to face work - a focus group approach - is very positive, particularly using a mini-questionnaire or framework to shape discussion.*

- *The focus group sessions can be used to create two-way listening (with students and parents) and generate constructive debate. Participants in the sessions enjoyed sharing similar problems in a supportive environment.*

Questionnaires

- *They give useful information but much more will come through discussions.*
- *There are problems of over use, coding and response rate.*
- *There are issues about how the information will be used.*

Imaging (Students' drawings)

A number of participants had experimented with student drawing. Staff from Cansfield Community High School Wigan presented findings from their experiment aimed at using students' drawings to their London colleagues. Using music and visual stimuli (the works of the painter Vassily Kandinsky), and encouraging students to draw and use colour to reflect their mood, they had worked with a group of disaffected students and had been successful in creating a stimulating learning environment and in discovering much about how the young people experience their school life. Reflections from this exercise included:

- *There are powerful insights from the approach, the colours are an effective way of understanding how students feel.*
- *The exercise generates a rich use of language in a group of students who are not typically seen as being particularly engaged in learning and provides opportunities for them to express themselves without the written word.*
- *Students take it very seriously and feel valued.*
- *The exercise helps to establish trust and rapport.*
- *As a methodology, it needs lots of trialing and it is important to have a clear framework.*

steps along the way

Triangulation (ie using a range of research methods)
- *Student discussion before giving them a questionnaire can be valuable.*
- *For parents, the questionnaire and discussion, generates a rich response.*
- *Discussion helps elucidate understanding of key terms such as "respect".*
- *By collecting data formally, i.e. through a structured questionnaire, it was possible to identify broad differences which would have been missed through discussion only.*

Final reflections on the research tools
- *What I've learned is that the environment matters more to disaffected kids than other children.*
- *There are others ways we could look at students' experience e.g. using digital cameras or student narratives.*
- *Using both qualitative and quantitative approaches reveals different data.*
- *We need to think about how to use tools in a democratic way.*

the benefits of collaboration
Staff have welcomed the opportunities to collaborate and the time and space to reflect energising and rewarding (see staff poster 3). This has enabled them to:

Share with colleagues
- *There is great creativity and knowledge among all the participants and a positive atmosphere for sharing ideas and learning about different approaches.*
- *There are high levels of expertise in the group and we can learn much from each other.*
- *There are many different ways of tackling these issues. Some I never would have thought of on my own.*

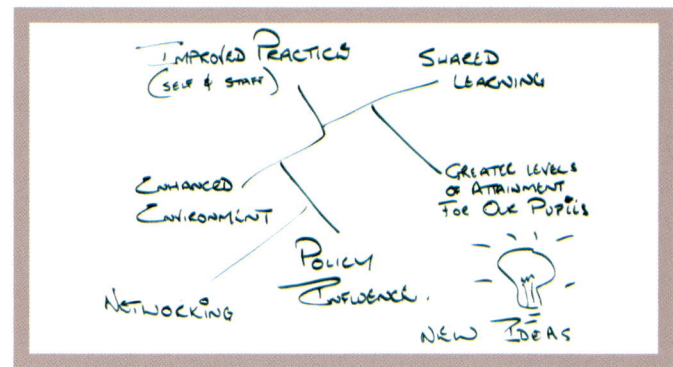

Staff Poster 3 : Collaborating for Change

- *It's great to find that I am not alone. We are all in the same boat.*
- *I have admiration for colleagues and for their determination to tackle the challenges.*
- *There is a large amount of energy and enthusiasm and a desire to take risks.*
- *Seeing what other people have done, what they have experienced and what we can take back is invigorating.*

Seeing things afresh
- *It's a relief that children are part of the discussion. Too often they are seen as the problem and not as central to the solutions.*
- *Hearing the students' voices, engaging them in the project and making them feel valued as individuals is how we will make this project work.*
- *We're thinking about what works for children, not how to jump exam hurdles. It's what I came into teaching to do.*
- *The workshop has provided space for thinking, away from everyday life, in a reflective atmosphere.*

steps along the way

Step 4 : Find out what students think

Each school team has developed its own way of finding out what students think. With the help of Dr Jim Docking, we have also developed a student questionnaire and had an 89% response rate (71 students). We found that:

- Females were more positive than males about wanting to go to school and were more likely than males to disagree that 'school is a waste of time'.
- While students tended to value school (4 out of 5) they didn't necessarily like it (1 out of 2).
- In general, students' feelings about school were mixed: there were some good and bad days, good and bad teachers (see chart 1).
- Comments within schools could differ markedly, for example, a student in one school wrote 'The same as every day - sleepy and can't wait to go home' while another commented 'So far this term I have had a good time'.
- While 1 in 2 students thought that if they were stuck in their school work, all or most teachers would help them, ONLY 1 in 5 thought that staff listened to them, or knew and understood them (see chart 2).

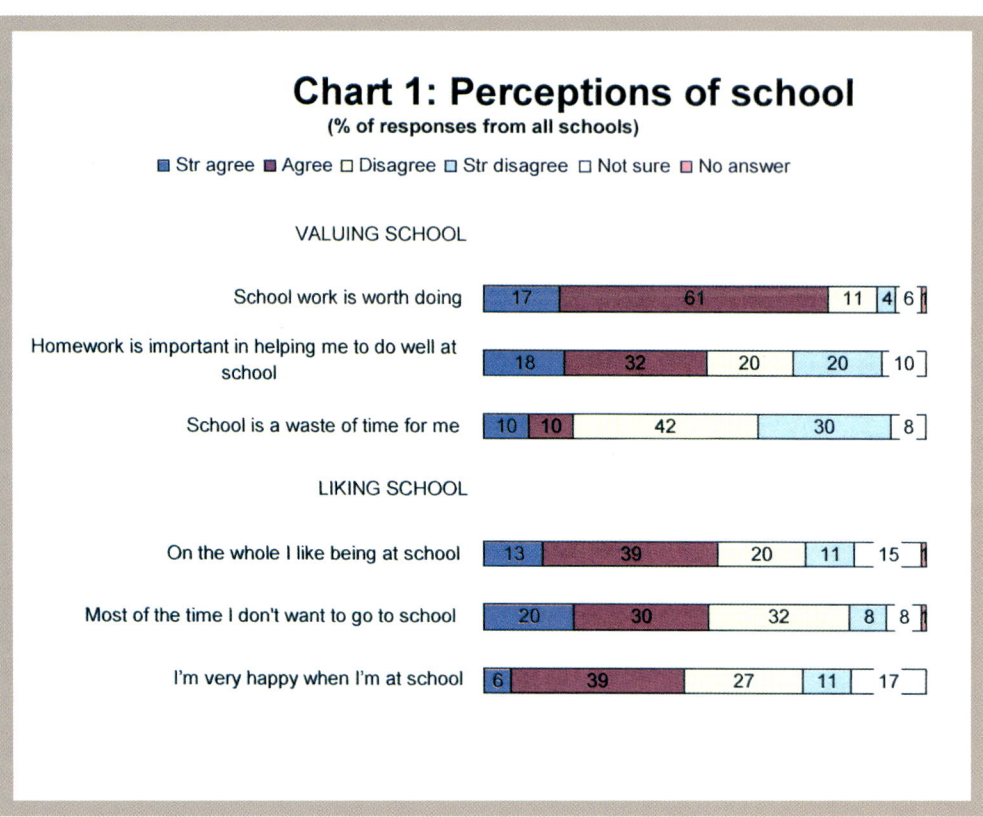

Chart 1 : Perceptions of School

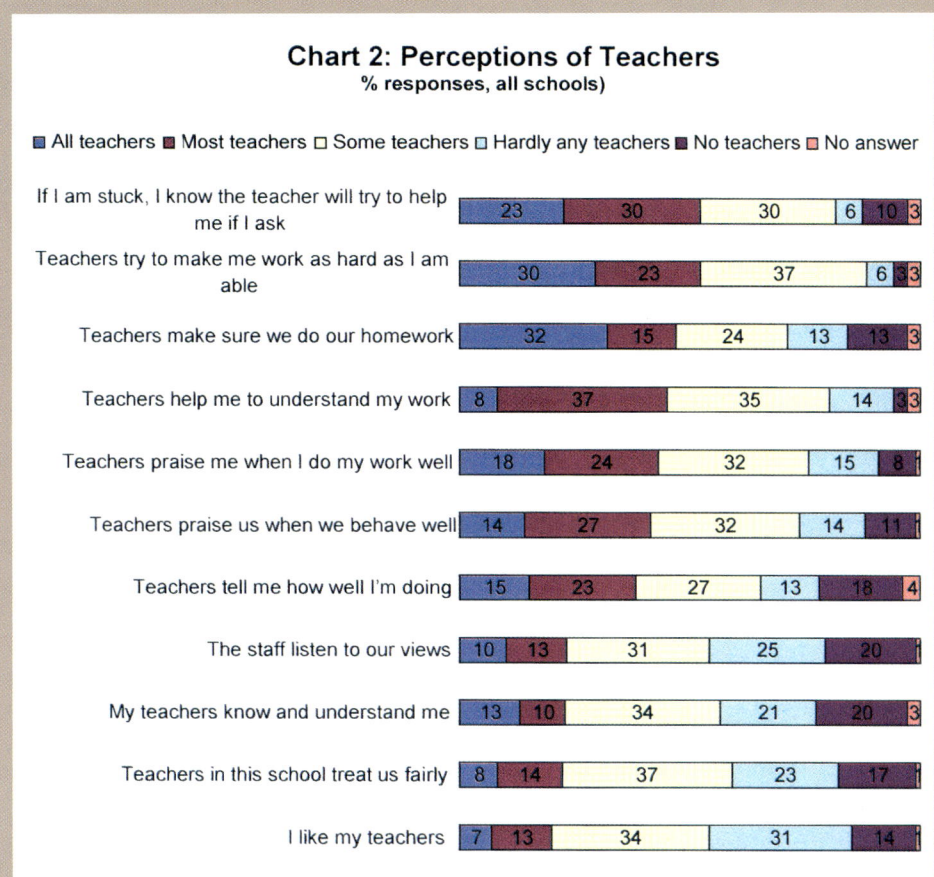

Chart 2: Perceptions of Teachers
% responses, all schools)

■ All teachers ■ Most teachers □ Some teachers □ Hardly any teachers ■ No teachers □ No answer

	All teachers	Most teachers	Some teachers	Hardly any teachers	No teachers	No answer
If I am stuck, I know the teacher will try to help me if I ask	23	30	30	6	10	3
Teachers try to make me work as hard as I am able	30	23	37	6	3	3
Teachers make sure we do our homework	32	15	24	13	13	3
Teachers help me to understand my work	8	37	35	14	3	3
Teachers praise me when I do my work well	18	24	32	15	8	
Teachers praise us when we behave well	14	27	32	14	11	
Teachers tell me how well I'm doing	15	23	27	13	18	4
The staff listen to our views	10	13	31	25	20	
My teachers know and understand me	13	10	34	21	20	3
Teachers in this school treat us fairly	8	14	37	23	17	
I like my teachers	7	13	34	31	14	

Chart 2 : Perceptions of Teachers

Relationships

For the students in our project, teacher-student relationships are critical. They are concerned about teachers who shout, nag, pick on individuals, or are unfair.

< *They could be less angry and could be more friendly.*
< *Yeah they can be a bit fair and help us a bit more.*

Lessons

The quality of lessons is also important. Students want lessons to be more interesting, more fun, and more supportive of their individual needs.

< *Loads of fun activities and lessons that are worth doing because some lessons are so much a waste of time.*
< *Make lessons more interesting and help us more and praise us for our work.*
< *Yes, make lessons more fun.*
< *Take us on more activities and trips.*
< *Give me more support and help.*
< *They could make it more interesting and more practical.*

Being taken account of

They also want their feelings and opinions to count for more, and to draw a more positive response from staff.

< *Yes, listen to me for a change.*
< *Listen when we're upset.*
< *Understand my views.*
< *Listen to us when we have something to say.*

steps along the way

steps along the way

Step 5 : Create new learning opportunities - inside and outside school

Inside school

Relationships with staff matter for all students and they matter even more for students on the margins. A key element of the strategy is to ensure that the students who are taking part in the project are well supported in school and have key teachers or learning mentors who know and understand them. Equally important is the space and opportunity for the students to come together as a group.

Henry Compton School has identified 15 Year 10 students, all boys, a mixed group with very different abilities and backgrounds. They value being in school but are often disengaged, struggling in a number of ways. The chosen boys are very enthusiastic as they feel that someone senior is now listening to them. They see themselves as the 'Challenge Group' and are offered support in class time. The goal is to raise attitudes and expectations.

As a group, Henry Compton boys have looked at what turns them off school, and they will have to decide on the six most important things that they want the staff to know. They are unhappy about practical things, such as the school canteen (not enough food!) and the lack of green space around the school, and wearied by the constant demands to write, arguing that teachers play it safe by asking them to write. Parents are enthusiastic about their sons' involvement in the project and the boys are currently working on a presentation for their parents.

Henry Compton

steps along the way

The Bridge Academy is a Pupil Referral Unit for students in Hammersmith and Fulham. The Academy has identified 15 Year 9 students, predominantly boys, with very different agendas and abilities.

In an effort to establish solidarity as a group, the Academy team took the young people to Nando's (their choice). As one of the team members reported:

We had a whale of a time while reinforcing the purpose of the group and the overall aims of the project. The time away from school, having fun, alleviated some of the fears and doubts some of the young people had. One interesting question that one of the young people raised was whether or not other students who were getting on with their education would be called 'affected' instead of 'disaffected'.

The team has met with a group of parents of the students, exploring experiences, opinions, concerns about disaffection. Parents are very pleased to have the opportunity to be involved in discussions about their children and what can be done to re-engage them in learning.

Bridge Academy

steps along the way

Thomas Tallis School has identified a group the "London Challenge Group", predominantly boys, selected because they are disaffected and don't like being at school. The aim is to find out what they don't like and what they want from the school experience. The group meets weekly with one of the teachers and have dropped the equivalent of one GCSE to create some space. They receive regular support and help with subjects and with any coursework they are struggling with.

The students came up with a list of rewards and treats that they would like as part of their bargain with the school: not to be late to lessons, not to be confrontational, to keep up with the work and not have any bad comments written into their planners. The reward system is operated on a strict point basis.

The group has relished the challenges at Margaret McMillan House and there have been marked changes in teachers' perceptions about them during extra curricular activities.

The challenge now is to transfer that level of positive engagement into the academic curriculum. The school is closely tracking the groups' achievement and behaviour across the whole curriculum and is beginning to identify areas in its current institutional practices that need closer focus.

Thomas Tallis

Eltham Green School have a group of 13 girls, selected specifically because they are very capable but are underachieving, and are becoming disaffected and have poor attendance. They are a mixed ability group and meet once a week in school time. The primary goal at Eltham Green is to raise their self-esteem. The girls are currently working on Powerpoint presentations about themselves and their aspirations which will be fed back to a wider group in the school, including staff. Comments in one Powerpoint included:

What I like about me...
I like to think I've got a nice heart but sometimes it is more or less in the wrong place.
What I hate about myself...
Sometimes I get really aggressive towards people but I don't mean it. I guess I'm just trying to fit in.
What I like about my school...
My mentors, they have always been there for me to sort out my problems. I really don't know how they put up with me sometimes.
What I hate about school...
Teachers think they are helping you by shouting at you but really they're not they are just causing you to react.

Staff teams have met with parents who are very supportive of the project. The girls have thrived at Margaret McMillan House, working together as a group, listening to each other, sharing their learning and supporting each other.

Kidbrooke School has identified 17 year 9 students (mainly boys) who are disaffected from school in different ways. The school doesn't know why the students find it so difficult, and are trying to find some answers and bridge the gap between school and after school, creating a link to what happens after they are 16.

One of the first tasks has been to get the students to complete a diary - "A day in the life of ...". This begins before school and goes through the whole of the school's day, including breaks and after school. It asks - What happened? How did it make me feel? It also asks - How could it have been a better day for you? and What could you have done today to make a difference?

The students plan to convey their observations in a range of ways, including using music and drama. Their time at MMH has boosted students' confidence and enabled them to recognise the good qualities in each other and to reflect on their own behaviour. The Kidbrooke team plans to develop a newsletter (which will help writing skills) and to work with parents, helping to break down the barriers that these parents have with school.

steps along the way

steps along the way

Outside school

A key question for the project team has been: if we change the learning environment will this help students to re-engage in learning in new ways? Given this question we began our partnership with Margaret McMillan House. We wanted to explore the ways in which an out-of-school, outdoor learning experience can enable young people to access learning in new and different ways.

At MMH, students are involved in a range of problem-solving and collaborative activities and are also supported by older student mentors from the Greenwich Schools and William Morris Academy - a highly successful strategy. We are building up their involvement at MMH incrementally.

Visit I (Autumn 04-Spring 05). One day visit to experience the 'Hub' and 'Anderson' Challenges. These are designed to encourage team based problem-solving and creativity, and to enhance student self-esteem. A primary goal of this first visit has been to encourage each school group of students to gel as a group. In their first visit students have concentrated on:

< Working Together - Communication;
< Doing Your Best - Motivation;
< Thinking Creatively and Safely;
< Completing the Task.

Kidbrooke Students

Visit 2 (Autumn 04-Spring 05). An overnight stay at MMH which has been designed to:

< Continue to work on the students' team-building skills;
< Continue supporting their personal development in terms of self-esteem, confidence and interpersonal skills;
< Extend the learning experiences of each individual and assist in re-engaging them with their learning environment;
< Connect their learning to their school experiences;
< Create opportunities to express feelings and ideas about their own learning in a pro-active way;
< Continue to foster good relationships with mentors, tutors and teachers in a fun and challenging way;
< Evaluate their learning experience through an art-based activity

feeling positive about self

undertaking new challenges

feeling of belonging to a team

SELF ESTEEM

Underpinning Elements

Kidbrooke Students

Visit 3 (Summer 05). Overnight camp at MMH.

Visit 4 (Autumn 05-Spring 06). Extended visit to Tyn-y-Berth Mountain Centre, Powys, which is linked to MMH.

A number of tools have been developed to evaluate the benefits to be gained from team work and from undertaking the new challenges at MMH. A particular focus is on students' self-esteem. We are also gathering qualitative data on students' own perceptions of what works for them as learners, and how the approaches that work for them could help them learn more effectively in school. The underpinning elements of the framework for analysis are shown above. There will be more about this in our next booklet.

steps along the way

steps along the way

Step 6 : Reflect on what we've learned

At every state in the project we are trying to reflect on what the students have learned and what we have learned as a project team.

There have been many gains from the Margaret McMillan House experience. Below summarises what we have seen so far.

- The students are articulate and reflective.
- The atmosphere encourages them to talk about each other constructively.
- Feedback develops empathy.
- The involvement of VI form mentors has been extremely important.
- The programme clearly has an impact.
- The experience helps develop group negotiation skills.
- There is evidence of students taking responsibility for their own behaviour.
- Staff perceptions of the students have changed : what they can do and how they can behave.
- The experience fosters kinaesthetic learning.
- It provides an opportunity for students to stick to an activity and try things out.

A summary of our approach

Step 1: Identify a core team of staff who want to explore new ways of working with students and develop a change strategy.

Step 2: Give staff time to share their aspirations.

Step 3: Give staff opportunities to experiment with a range of research tools and work together.

Step 4: Find out what students think.

Step 5: Create new learning opportunities - inside and outside school.

Step 6: Reflect on what we've learned.

What do students have to say?

Schools have asked their students for their views about the project so far. What they have gained from being a part of the project? What had they gained from being a part of the Challenge Group? How has it influenced their views about themselves, or their thoughts about their own learning?

Students from Eltham Green school commented as follows...

I honestly believe that its made me discover the real me rather than the fake me. I used to put on a fake me to impress people but now I know the real me is good.

It teaches us how to communicate properly and you can talk to other people and share ideas in lessons.

When I was at MMH it made me work with other people, not just on my own like I usually do. I can come to school without keeping all my problems in and getting my stresses out so I can concentrate on my work.

The London Challenge helps me with my lessons because when I feel I can't work cos I'm tired, I remember the things we learnt on how to stimulate your mind and I can get twice the work done.

Yes because we talk about school and stuff and it's made me realise how important school is.

We can't work properly and if we've got problems in our mind, the group work helps us unload.

It teaches me not to give up and to face some of the challenges.

While most have been very positive, one or two remain to be convinced.

Don't know. It might teach me to work in groups and control my anger.

No, school is crap.

We have few doubts of the overall benefits or the approach we are developing. It's been fun for students and for staff too (see staff poster 4). We hope that as the project continues, we will be able to convince all of the students of the benefits, as well as staff in all of the schools.

Eltham Green Girls

what next?

What next?

There is still much to do in the project and we see the biggest challenges as:

Maintaining the momentum: Staff in the schools involved in this project have many commitments, many demands on their time and energy. The students we are working with can become discouraged by a range of factors outside the remit of the project.

Transferring the learning: We have been able to demonstrate that students who are often seen as poor learners in school can become creative and collaborative learners in a different environment. We will need to find ways of transferring our learning into the school curriculum, and into schools' day-to-day practices.

Demonstrating that this approach can be embraced by other schools: The London Challenge funding for this project has created opportunities to experiment, to reflect and to work together. We will need to find ways of supporting innovation which will enable the approaches developedin the project to be adopted and used by schools without the same level of support.

Further Resources
A range of materials about the project are being developed, including a video on the project (available July 2005).

ME REACH MY FULL POTENTIAL AS A TEACHER AND LEARNER AND HAVE FUN ☺

AND FOR PUPILS AND TEACHERS EVERYWHERE

Staff Poster 4: Fun and Learning for staff and students

Tallis student and staff